The Beauty Book

Other Books Available in The Lily Series

Fiction

Here's Lily!
Lily Robbins, MD (Medical Dabbler)—coming soon!

Nonfiction

The Body Book—coming soon!

The Beauty Book

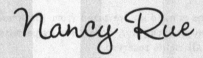

Nancy Rue

A Division of Thomas Nelson Publishers

NASHVILLE DALLAS MEXICO CITY RIO DE JANEIRO

The Beauty Book
© 2012 Nancy Rue

Published in association with the literary agency of Alive
Communications, Inc., 7680 Goddard Street, Suite 200, Colorado Springs,
CO 80920. www.alivecommunications.com

Published in Nashville, Tennessee, by Tommy Nelson®. Tommy Nelson is a
registered trademark of Thomas Nelson, Inc.

Thomas Nelson, Inc., titles may be purchased in bulk for educational,
business, fund-raising, or sales promotional use. For information, please
e-mail SpecialMarkets@ThomasNelson.com.

Library of Congress Cataloging-in-Publication Data

Rue, Nancy N.
  The beauty book / Nancy Rue.
      p. cm. -- (The Lily series)
  ISBN 978-1-4003-1948-0 (pbk.)
1. Girls--Religious life--Juvenile literature. 2. Beauty, Personal--
Religious aspects--Christianity--Juvenile literature. 3. Body, Human--
Religious aspects--Christianity--Juvenile literature. 4. Self-perception
in children--Juvenile literature.. 5. Self-perception--Religious aspects--
Christianity--Juvenile literature. I. Title.
  BV4551.3.R83 2012
  248.8'2--dc23

                                                2012004688

Printed in the United States of America
12 13 14 15 16 QG 6 5 4 3 2 1

www.thomasnelson.com

Contents

One

You Gotta Love It

LORD, you are our Father.
We are the clay, you are the potter;
we are all the work of your hand.

ISAIAH 64:8

You Gotta Love It

Okay, let's get one fact straight right up front: every girl has her own special beauty.

Yeah, I know you've heard your mom say, "Well, *I* think you're beautiful, honey." I also know that doesn't mean a whole bunch when some kid's calling you Pizza Face or everybody's telling your sister she's drop-dead gorgeous and then patting you on the head and saying, "You're cute too, honey."

But really, God doesn't make junk. He made each of us just exactly the way He intends us to be. So just like everything else God made—from blackberries to rhinoceroses—*you gotta love it*. You gotta love *you* too.

"Yeah," you may ask, *"but if every girl is beautiful, how come "everybody" isn't seeing it that way?"*

Because—bummer!—people aren't like God. Somewhere along the way, since the whole Adam and Eve thing, somebody decided there was only one way to be a beautiful woman at any given time. Right now that standard is being five foot ten, weighing about a hundred pounds, and having lips as big as the living room couch.

So how are you supposed to convince "everybody" that you're this knockout even though God shaped you like a fire hydrant or gave you lips the width of a pencil line or gave you curves nobody else has at ten?

You can't. You only need to convince *you*, and that's what this book is about. By the time you get to the end, I want you to be able to check yourself out when you pass a store window and say, "That's me. Cool! And I love that!"

Here's a good way to start. From now until you finish reading this book, try to follow this rule: NO BAD-MOUTHING THE WAY YOU LOOK.

That means no dwelling on the zits that have appeared on your forehead. No talking about how fat you think you are. No wishing you had curlier hair (or smaller ears or straighter teeth). Pretend you are one of your friends. You would rather eat brussels sprouts than hurt a friend's feelings, right? So NO putting your friend—*you!*—down.

That's a really hard rule to follow, so let's look at some of the things that can keep you from seeing how gorgeous you are.

BEAUTY BLOCKER #1: TV TRAINING

One of the reasons people think there's only one way to be beautiful is because that's all they see on television and in magazines and movies and on the Internet. Even the Barbie dolls seem to scream, "You have to look like me!" But you don't.

GIRLZ Want to Know

❀ *LILY: Those girls on the cover of* Seventeen *have perfect skin. How do they get that?*

They don't. Nobody's skin is that perfect. Everybody has at least the occasional zit, freckle, or scar from when she crashed her bike. Those magazine photos are retouched with computer programs and digital editing software that can remove "blemishes" (why don't they just call them pimples?), make eyelashes longer, and even chisel in great cheekbones. If you met those models in person, you would see that they have pimples, birthmarks, and little scars too. No lie.

❀ *ZOOEY: If I use the shampoos and face creams I see in the ads, will I look the way the models do?*
Probably not. For starters, that model isn't you. And don't you think if a company wants to sell a product that's supposed to give you thick, shiny hair, they're going to pick a model who *already has* that thick, shiny hair? Besides, if you were born with thin hair, there isn't much in this world that's going to make it thick. But who says you have to have thick hair to be beautiful?

❀ *RENI: I'm the shrimpiest girl in my whole class. Why does God even make short girls when tall girls are always the ones people think are beautiful?*
Actually, people's ideas of what's beautiful change over time. Back in the late 1500s and early 1600s, plump women with rolls of rosy flesh were considered beautiful, mostly because the better fed you were, the wealthier that meant you were. In the 1950s, lots of curves were the going thing in the movies and on the posters. By today's standards, Marilyn Monroe would have been considered overweight, but men in the fifties drooled over full-figured women. In the 1960s, when the Beatles said on the radio that they preferred petite girls, everybody wanted to be a short little peanut.

Does that mean somebody who *was* beautiful forty, fifty, or four hundred years ago *wouldn't* be beautiful today? How much sense does *that* make? Nah, *this* makes sense: everyone has beauty—plump and rosy, round and curvy, short and pixie-like, *and* tall and pencil slim, not to mention everything in between.

BEAUTY BLOCKER #2: THE COMPARISON GAME

Come on. We've all played it.

"I don't have breasts yet, so I'm not as grown-up as Chelsea, but at least I don't have to wear those geeky braces like Whitney, so I can't be *that* bad."

It seems like a harmless enough game. After all, most of the time you just play it in your mind until you come out ahead of somebody and can make yourself feel better, right? Well . . . hmm. Let's see what God has to say about that.

How Is This a *God Thing*?

It used to be the "thing" to wear bracelets and T-shirts that said *WWJD: What Would Jesus Do?* You could even get it on boxer shorts, for Pete's sake! The trend has passed, but the question is still worth asking: What *would* Jesus do when faced with the temptation to make Himself feel like He was okay by playing the comparison game? Would He say to Himself, "Yikes! I don't have big muscles like Peter, so I must be pretty wimpy. Then again, Peter's always asking stupid questions. I must be smarter than he is. That's more important, right, Dad?"

Of *course* Jesus would never say that because Jesus was perfect. We will never be perfect, but we do try to be more like Him, right? And if the above is too lame for Jesus, it's too lame for us too. Dad, uh, *God* certainly doesn't compare us. Can you imagine God saying, "I sure did a great job on Carly's complexion. Too bad I messed up on Emily's. She's not nearly as cute." *Hello!*

God doesn't compare us. Jesus doesn't compare us. The world we live in compares us, but who are we supposed to follow?

Jesus made it really plain. Love your neighbor as yourself (check out Mark 12:31). That means no putting your "neighbor" down—and no putting yourself down. Period.

√ CHECK YOURSELF OUT

Each statement below has four possible endings. Circle the number next to the ending that fits you *best* in each group. Be *honest*. No fair picking the answer you think is "right." (What would you learn from that?)

A. *When it comes to height in my class,*

   4 I know right off the bat exactly how many people are taller and how many people are shorter than I am.

   3 I'd have to think about where I fall.

   2 I couldn't figure it out if you paid me.

   1 I don't care.

B. If you're talking complexion,

4 I have one of the best (or worst) in the class.

3 Now that you mention it, I do know how mine compares to other people's in my class.

2 I don't know—I've never thought about it.

1 I don't want to think about it.

C. When I think about hair,

4 I know I have more (or less) bad hair days than most people in my class.

3 Well . . . hmm . . . let me think.

2 Who cares about other people's hair?

1 Do people in my class have hair?

D. If somebody brought a scale to class,

4 I'd weigh bunches more (or less) than anybody else; I'm sure of it.

3 I guess I know where I'd fall, but I'd have to see everybody else's weight written down.

2 Why? Is somebody fat or something?

1 Don't know; don't even worry about it.

E. Can we talk—about chests?

4 I'm convinced I have the biggest (or smallest) one in class.

3 Come to think of it, I guess mine is one of the bigger (or smaller, or more average) ones in class.

2 I'd have to get out a tape measure.

1 I care about this because . . . ?

F. Klutzy? Clumsy? Me?

4 I'm the most (or least) clumsy person in the class. I don't even have to think about it.

3 It's not something I think about a whole lot, but, yeah, I fit onto the klutz scale somewhere.

2 What's a klutz?

1 Why are we even talking about this?

G. If I had to rate myself for overall appearance in comparison to my classmates,

4 I would put myself way at the top (or bottom) of the list without a second thought.

3 Gee, if I really put my mind to it, I could probably decide.

2 I guess it all depends on what you consider beautiful.

1 I have better things to do.

Use the key below to score yourself and add up your points. Then read what you've just discovered about yourself.

If you scored between 28 and 22 points, you qualify for the Olympic Games of Comparison! You may be making yourself unhappy by constantly measuring yourself against other people. Next time you feel yourself doing that, try paying the person you're comparing yourself to a compliment, and then thank God for what you look like and move on!

If you scored between 21 and 15 points, you are a newbie at the Comparison Game, but you'll play if somebody suggests it. Have you had conversations like this?

YOUR FRIEND: Do you think Susie Schmo is prettier than I am?

YOU: No way! Her teeth are way bigger than yours, and besides, she has a pig nose.

If you find yourself being pulled into a conversation like that, you might want to have an answer ready so you can pull yourself out, like this:

YOUR FRIEND: Do you think Susie Schmo is prettier than I am?
YOU: I don't play that game. Monopoly? Checkers? Those I'll play.

Warning! Your friend will probably think you're trying to dodge the "truth" that Susie Schmo really *is* prettier, but you can get *that* out of her head by paying her a compliment that doesn't compare her to Susie or anybody else. Something like this:

YOUR FRIEND: So you *do* think she's prettier than I am?
YOU: Your hair is amazing, you've got a smile to die for, and yikes—the dimples, girl, the dimples.

She'll have forgotten all about Susie Schmo by that time!

If you scored between 14 and 18, you're probably going, *What?* at all this talk of comparing. It just doesn't occur to you to compare people's appearances, and you wouldn't know where to start if it did. Be glad, but be careful. People, even your friends, may try to drag you into it:

YOUR FRIEND: Do you think Susie Schmo is prettier than I am?

YOU: Huh?

YOUR FRIEND: Susie Schmo. Do you think she has
   better hair than I have?

YOU: Hair? I don't know. I never thought about it.

YOUR FRIEND: Well, think about it!

And what comes next?

YOU: Nope. Sorry. That's not my thing.

If you scored a 7, congratulations! You not only don't
compare people's beauty, but it really ticks you off when
other people do it and try to make you do it. Keep it up. God
likes that about you.

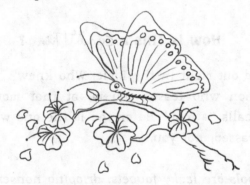

BEAUTY BLOCKER #3: THE TEASER

Whether it's your little brother, your grandpa, or those girls
at the other end of your lunch table, if somebody teases you
about the way you look, it can twist your image of yourself.
Even when you know the person is "just kidding" and says,
"Seriously, can't you take a joke?" stuff like this can hurt:

- "Hey, Jody, when's the Breast Fairy going to come
  visit you?"

- "Yikes, Sarah! With feet like that, who needs swim fins, right?"
- "How you doin', Chubby?"

Maybe you usually give one of these answers to teasing:

- "I'm just glad I don't have a chest like yours, Dolly Parton."
- "I don't have big feet! What are you talking about?"
- "Oh, shut up!"

But none of those responses will help you with your image of yourself and your own beauty. God, as usual, has a better way to deal with teasing.

How Is This a *God Thing*?

It's spelled out right in the Bible. Who knew?

A person who teases you is, at that moment, what Proverbs calls "a fool." He or she is the one who ought to be embarrassed, not you.

> *Fools are leaky faucets, dripping nonsense.*
> PROVERBS 15:2 MSG

> *All they do is run off at the mouth.*
> PROVERBS 18:2 MSG

Don't try to argue with a teaser.

> *Don't bother talking sense to fools;*
> *they'll only poke fun at your words.*
> PROVERBS 23:9 MSG

Don't join in either. You're just as much of a "fool" if you tease back.

> *The start of a quarrel is like a leak in a dam,*
> *so stop it before it bursts.*
> PROVERBS 17:14 MSG

Whatever you do, don't get mad and turn it into a fight.

> *A gentle response defuses anger,*
> *but a sharp tongue kindles a temper-fire.*
> PROVERBS 15:1 MSG

Let teasers who aren't friends or family know what you think of their behavior—by *ignoring* them.

> *Don't respond to the stupidity of a fool;*
> *you'll only look foolish yourself.*
> PROVERBS 26:4 MSG

If the teaser is someone in your family or a close friend, tell that person that teasing hurts you. Honesty is always best in a relationship. You can tell him or her:

> *Words kill, words give life;*
> *they're either poison or fruit—you choose.*
> PROVERBS 18:21 MSG

Try to remember this about teasing: it just flat out isn't *true!*

> *You have as little to fear from an undeserved curse*
> *as from the dart of a wren or the swoop of a swallow.*
> PROVERBS 26:2 MSG

By the way, if you are a teaser, remember this:

If you are dumb enough to call attention to yourself
by offending people and making rude gestures,
don't be surprised if someone bloodies your nose.

PROVERBS 30:32 MSG

Finding the You-nique You

We've talked about what *not* to do:

❀ Don't be influenced by the media (TV, magazines, etc.).
❀ Don't play the Comparison Game.
❀ Don't let teasing twist your mind.

But *how* are you supposed to believe that you're the beautiful young woman God made you to be when everyone else is telling you you're *not?*

You do it by discovering your own special beauty. You figure out what is *unique* about your appearance—what makes you one of a kind, what makes you *you.*

Let's go on a search for the "you-nique you."

√ CHECK YOURSELF OUT

Take this quiz in front of the biggest mirror you can find. While looking at yourself in the mirror and remembering that the girl you see there is your friend, complete the sentences below. There are two rules for your answers:

RULE #1: Your answer has to be honest.
RULE #2: Your answer has to be a compliment.

Example:
Her hair is the stringiest stuff on the planet. (NO!)
Her hair is long and wispy and soft. (YES!)

Are you in front of your mirror? Here we go.

Her (that's you!) hair is _____.
Her forehead is _____.
Her ears are _____.
Her eyebrows are _____.
Her eyes are _____.
Her nose is _____.
Her complexion is _____.
Her cheeks are _____.
Her mouth is _____.

Her smile is _____.

Her chin is _____.

Her height is _____.

Her arms are _____.

Her legs are _____.

Now read your statements out loud, one after the other, as if you're reading about a character in a book, or better yet, about your friend.

Try to come up with one statement that describes this whole *you*. Like . . .

This girl sounds cute, like a little elf with wonderful, one-of-a-kind ears!

or . . .

This girl is a healthy, wholesome-looking angel!

This girl (YOU!) is _____.

Just Do It

Now your job is to *believe* that statement—every day, all the time. You are uniquely beautiful in the way you've just described. You didn't make it up; it was there right in front of you. Try one of these ways to remind yourself that it's true:

- Keep your description of yourself in a place where you can read it often (and where your brother can't get hold of it!).
- Are you artistic? Draw a picture of "this girl," following your written description exactly. Keep your drawing where you can see *you* every day.
- Every time you hear yourself saying or thinking, *My legs are so fat,* or *My hair is out of control,* toss that thought out and replace it with something you wrote, such as, *My legs are really smooth.*

- When you pray, thank God, item by item, for the *you* you've described: "Thank You, Father, for my chocolate-chip-brown eyes and my two straight front teeth that make my smile so bright and my long, thin arms that will probably never be flabby." God wants to know that you appreciate everything He's done for you.

God-Confidence

Now that you're starting to be convinced that you *are* beautiful, let's look at another very important part of this.

Have you ever known a girl who looked like she just came off the cover of *Seventeen*? One who never had to worry about anyone saying, "My hair (or anything else!) looks better than hers"? Who was never teased about any part of her whole self?

And who was so hateful that sometimes she was downright ugly to look at?

Or have you ever known a girl who maybe had some big-time funky things about her appearance? Maybe she was cross-eyed or had buck teeth. But the more you got to know her, the prettier she seemed, because not only was she nice to everyone, but she was nice to herself too.

The reason? You look good when you are good. You look beautiful when you are sure of yourself. A lot of people call that *self-confidence*. But really? It's *God-confidence*.

√ CHECK YOURSELF OUT

See for yourself. Get in front of that mirror again. Smile at that girl as if you like her and accept her and want to be BFFs. Now watch what happens when you look at her as if you hate her guts. Which girl looks better?

How Is This a *God Thing*?

You can have that God-confidence that makes you beautiful because . . .

- God carefully chose each of your features and combined them to make *you*.
- God's idea of you is perfect, even if what's hot for models right now doesn't agree.
- Jesus only ever talked about inner beauty. If you've got Him, you've got that, baby! Now think about *that* and look in the mirror. You gotta love it.

Talking to God About It

If you're like a lot of girls, what we've talked about in this chapter is probably new stuff, some really different ways of thinking about *you*. How are you ever going to remember it all?

Relax! You don't have to do it on your own. That's what God's here for, to help you. All you have to do is ask.

Write a prayer about the things you want to remember about being the you-nique, beautiful you. Fill in the blanks below if you want, or write your own prayer.

Dear _____ (your favorite name for God),
    I'm discovering that I'm beautiful—because
You made me that way. But sometimes it's hard
for me to remember and believe that because
_____. I especially have a hard
time thinking of my _____ as
beautiful. Will You please help me not to pay attention

to what TV and magazines say is beautiful, especially
_____? Will You please help me not
to play the Comparison Game, especially about or
with _____? And, Lord, please help
me deal with _____ teasing about
my _____. Most of all, God, help
me remember that You love me, that You made me
perfect, and that I can have the God-confidence that
makes me you-niquely different from everyone else.

I love You, God! _____ (your name)

Lily Pad

The time I felt the absolute prettiest was when . . .

Two

Heads Up!

"Even the very hairs of your head are all numbered."

MATTHEW 10:30

How Is Hair a *God Thing*?

One of the things God wants us to do is make the very most of what He's given us. You are the *most* beautiful when you're taking care of your temple—that's your physical self.

What better place to start than with your hair? Hey, if your "crowning glory" isn't glorious, you aren't going to feel as beautiful as you truly are.

Here's to Your Hair Health

Before we even *think* about hair dryers and flat irons and French braids, we have to talk about healthy hair. If your hair's "sick," it isn't going to look great no matter what else you do to it.

Just Do It

Take a look at your hair habits. Answer these questions, and of course, be honest.

1. How often do you wash your hair?
Your hair might be looking greasier as you're getting older because the glands that produce oil are making more of it now. The best guideline is to wash your hair whenever it starts to look stringy or feel oily. For most girls, that's several times a week. For way active girls and those with lots of oil, washing your hair every day is a good idea.

2. What kind of shampoo do you use?
Is it made especially for your hair type (dry, normal, oily, fine, curly)? Check the label. Shampoo that is formulated

for your hair type will give you a head start (hee hee) on a great 'do every day.

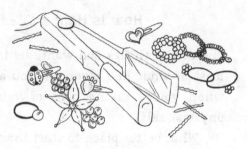

3. How much shampoo do you use?

A "serving" about the size of a quarter in the palm of your hand is a good guideline.

4. Do you get all the tangles out of your hair before you wash it?

You definitely should. It will make shampooing it thoroughly and combing it out later much easier.

5. How do you scrub your hair?

After you've spread your quarter-size helping of shampoo evenly over your wet hair, work it in all the way to your roots, but don't scratch at your scalp with your fingernails. Just massage with your fingertips. Scrub harder—but still don't scratch—around your entire hairline. If your hair is really oily, be extra gentle with the massage so you don't encourage all those oil glands to start working overtime.

6. Do you rinse your hair until there's no more shampoo coming out of it?

Shampoo left in your hair will make it dry and dull.

7. Do you use conditioner on your hair?

Not everybody needs to. Use conditioner if

- your hair gets really tangled when you wash it;
- your hair is way dry;

• your hair's been damaged, maybe from coloring it or using curling irons, flat irons, or blow-dryers a lot.

8. How much conditioner do you use?

Use just enough to put on the ends of your hair, and try to use conditioner to match your hair type. If you use too much, your hair will be limp and so soft that you won't be able to do fun things with it. It might get greasy faster too.

9. How often do you have your hair cut or trimmed?

If you answered, "Never! I want my hair to grow way long!" or, "I don't know—whenever it starts to look stupid, I guess," you might want to know this—it's best to have your hair trimmed every six to eight weeks to get rid of split ends and to keep your style, well, *style-able*. If you want long, healthy hair, get a trim on schedule, and let it grow. If your head is a nest of split ends, it'll never get longer. Honest.

Anybody's hair can be healthy, and healthy hair means you'll have your own personal bounce and shine.

You've Got Style, Girl!

Remember when we talked about the you-nique you? That really applies to the hairstyle you choose. A 'do you like on somebody else might not be the best one for you. But there *is* a style that's perfect for you.

√ CHECK YOURSELF OUT

Check the answer under each statement that best describes you.

1. *When I run my hands through my hair, it feels*
   - ❀ thin and fine
   - ❀ sort of medium
   - ❀ thick
   - ❀ I can't run my hands through my hair!

Be sure your hair can do what you're asking it to do. A way thick mane of tight, curly hair isn't going to cascade down your back, and very fine hair will have a hard time holding curls and might not be happy in a French braid.

2. *My personality (most of the time) is*
   - ❀ bubbly
   - ❀ mature for my age
   - ❀ dreamy and quiet
   - ❀ sporty
   - ❀ artistic
   - ❀ studious

Be sure the style you're thinking about is *you*. Are you going for little curls all around your face when a sleek ponytail matches your let's-play-soccer personality? That doesn't mean you can't "try on" different versions of *you*, but for your everyday 'do, you'll want to be comfortable under your hair.

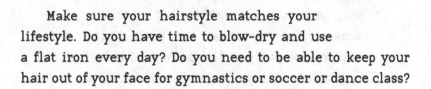

3. *My lifestyle is:*
   ❀ I have a lot of free time.
   ❀ I'm pretty busy, but I'm really active.
   ❀ I'm super busy.
   ❀ I'm pretty much a couch potato in my free time.

Make sure your hairstyle matches your lifestyle. Do you have time to blow-dry and use a flat iron every day? Do you need to be able to keep your hair out of your face for gymnastics or soccer or dance class?

4. *I would best describe my body type as*
   ❀ tiny and pixie-like. (Beware of too-big hair that wears you!)
   ❀ short, round, and cuddly. (Don't let your hair be round too, or you'll get lost in there!)
   ❀ somewhere in the middle. (Nothing too extreme is best.)
   ❀ tall and willowy. (Try not to let your hair be droopy.)
   ❀ like a big, wonderful teddy bear. (Steer away from busy 'dos or those cut really close to your head.)
   ❀ sturdy, strong, and powerfully square. (Best not to wear your hair too severe. Go soft.)

Now brush your hair back so you can see the shape and size of your face. If it's okay with the grown-ups, use the corner of a bar of soap or a dry-erase marker (not a permanent one!) to trace that shape on a mirror.

5. *Is the shape you've drawn*

❀ round? Long and straight works with your wonderfully soft face. So does some height on top and fullness at the sides. Short and curly can be fun, but just know that it will give you a cherub look.

❀ square? How classy! Make the most of that very sophisticated face shape with your hair cut either above or below your jaw line but not right at it. Nothing too puffy at the corners of your forehead or jaw line either.

❀ long? A long face is so dramatic and exotic. You won't want to pile hair up on top of your head, but go ahead and fluff it out at the sides.

❀ triangle- or pear-shaped? That's a face with interest and character. Experiment with different types of bangs. Play with angles, but keep it smooth at your jaw line.

❀ heart-shaped? How romantic. Curls or fluffiness at your jaw line is perfect. You won't want a lot of puff on top though.

❀ oval? Just about anything goes for you. Try new things. You can hardly go wrong.

Things to Remember When You're Stylin'

🌸 Never brush wet hair because it will break easily.
Use a wide-tooth comb or a pick to get out tangles,
and don't go after them like you're raking the lawn!
Start with the ends, and slowly work your way up.

🌸 Use a brush with round tips on the bristles or a
brush with natural bristles—they're the easiest on
your hair.

🌸 Clean your brushes and combs once a week. First
remove any hair from the brushes with your comb,
and then wash them all with—what else?—shampoo!

🌸 Don't share combs and brushes. It's kind of like
lending or borrowing a toothbrush. *Eww!*

🌸 Blow-dryers, curling irons, and flat irons can
really dry out your hair and leave you with a head
full of frizzy straw. Use your blow-dryer on the
lowest setting, and try not to use curling irons
or flat irons every day. (Also, spritzing on a little
heat protection spray before you begin styling can
save those beautiful tresses.)

🌸 Mousse, styling creme, and thickening sprays give
your hair body if it's thin and fine, but use just a
little bit. If you dollop it on like whipped cream,
your hair will look stiff and will probably end up
being flat.

🌸 Gel is fun for "special effects," when you don't
care if your hair looks a little stiffer or spikier.

🌸 Hair spray helps hold your style and keep your
hair from flying all over the place, but again, a
little goes a long way. It can take the shine out of
your hair.

Hair Hassles:
GIRLZ Want to Know

✿ *SUZY: I swim in a pool almost every day. Is the chlorine bad for my hair? Will my hair turn green?*
Chlorine can give blond hair a greenish tint. It can also dry out anybody's hair. Here are some tips:

- Wet your hair with non-chlorine water before you get into the pool. Wet hair absorbs less chlorine.
- Rinse the chlorine out of your hair right after you've finished swimming.
- There is special shampoo for swimmers, but regular shampoo often works just as well.

✿ *KRESHA: I keep getting white flakes on my shoulders from my hair. Gross! What are they?*
If your scalp feels dry and itchy, you might have dandruff, which is not gross. It's just a common condition you can get rid of by using a special dandruff shampoo from the drugstore or from your doctor. Before you try a dandruff shampoo though, ask yourself if you've been using a lot of mousse, hair spray, or gel and haven't washed your hair every day. Those products can build up and cause itching and flakes that will go away with regular shampooing.

✿ *LILY: My little brother thought he'd be cute and stick gum in my hair. How do I get that out?*
Spread some peanut butter on that wad o' gum, and work it through until the gum comes out. Then wash the peanut butter out of your hair, of course!

🌸 *ZOOEY: My hair is, like, falling out! Every time I brush it, a bunch of hair is left in my brush! Am I going to go bald?*
You can probably relax—and you should since you lose less hair when you're relaxed. Most people lose about a hundred hairs a day. Since you have about *one hundred thousand* hairs growing from your scalp, you'll still have plenty at the end of the day! Of course, if you notice actual bald spots, tell a grown-up.

🌸 *RENI: I'm African American, you know, and my hair just breaks all the time.*
God made black girls' hair totally unique and especially fragile. Try not to use picks or other sharp tools, but rather use tools and products created specifically for your hair (there should be a section devoted to your special hair on the hair care aisle). If you use a straightener or a curl-relaxer, always use a conditioner afterward. Have your mom give you a hot oil treatment now and then.

Talking to God About It: Hair Prayer

I can almost hear you saying, "Does God really want to talk about my *hair*?" God wants to talk about anything that stands between you and Him and anything that makes you the *you* He has in mind. That includes your hair.

So as you get ready to pray today, check the subjects below that you—the you-nique you—want to talk with God about. Of course, add any I've left out, and use your own words to go to God with what's on your mind (or on your hair!).

I want to talk to God about:

* 🌼 the way I feel about my hair. I still think it's ugly, and I know that's wrong.
* 🌼 the fact that I stress way too much about my hair. I have a bad hair day and I freak out.
* 🌼 my not caring how I look. I forget to comb my hair half the time, or I fight with my mom about washing it or getting it cut.
* 🌼 how my mom won't let me wear my hair the way I want. I know I'm supposed to honor my parents, but . . . help!
* 🌼 being thankful for every hair on my head, just the way it is!

Lily Pad

If God talked about my hair, I bet He'd say . . .

Three

The Skinny on Skin

This is now . . . flesh of my flesh; she shall be called "woman."

GENESIS 2:23

It's Gotta Be Healthy

Along with your hair, your skin is the physical part of you that needs the most care if you're going to be the most beautiful you-nique you. That figures since your skin is your body's biggest organ. But yikes, it can be confusing!

GIRLZ Want to Know

❀ *ZOOEY: My mom dragged me to the makeup counter at the mall, and the lady said we needed all these cleansers and toners and serums and moisturizer thingies. I got so confused! Do I really need all that stuff?*

All you need to do right now is keep your face clean, moisturized, and protected from sun damage. Wash it when you get up and before you go to bed with a mild facial soap or facial cleanser. Don't use a deodorant bar or the body scrub you use for the rest of your body. Apply it with your hands or a soft washcloth. Rinse with warm—*not hot!*—water. That's all. (And if you're in a time pinch, those premoistened facial cleansing wipes are a great option.)

❀ *LILY: My skin is so white it practically blinds people! I know the sun is bad for your skin, but can't I get just a little tan to give me some color?*

Actually, no. What's wrong with white skin? Or any other shade of skin God gave you? There is no such thing as a safe tan. Period. The end. No ifs, ands, or buts. The sun (or a tanning bed) damages everybody's skin and can give you:

- early wrinkles
- brown spots

- burns
- allergic reactions
- skin cancer—and not just when you're "old"

The only "safe tan" is a sunless tan from a bottle, and truthfully, it can be really hard to apply evenly unless you go to a spray booth. And seriously, who has the time and money for that when there's absolutely nothing wrong with creamy-white skin?

❀ *LILY: Does that mean I'm never supposed to go out in the sun?*

No! The sun also provides vitamin D, which is very good for you. Just protect yourself:

- Wear sunscreen with an SPF (sun protection factor) of at least 30. That basically means the sunscreen will protect your skin thirty times longer than if you don't use anything. Apply sunscreen especially between ten in the morning and three in the afternoon, but to be on the safe side, use it all the time because the sun's rays are always dangerous, even when it's cloudy or cold.
- If you're out in the sun longer than a few hours, put on more sunscreen.
- Put on sunscreen again after you've been in the water. Every time!

- When you aren't swimming, cover up with a shirt and a hat.
- Go for the shade whenever you can.
- Don't feel like a wimp for protecting yourself. You're just making sure you won't end up looking like a piece of luggage or having skin cancer.

❀ SUZY: *That's it? Just wash your face and make sure you're protected when you're in the sun?*

Basically. And get enough sleep, eat a healthy diet, get plenty of exercise, and drink lots of water. If you're not sure what a healthy diet is or how much exercise is good, read *The Body Book*.

Face Flaws!

It seems like just when you really start to care about how you look—*bam!*—your skin breaks out and you think you look like a pepperoni pizza. Or you get a big ol' cold sore that resembles a raspberry hanging off your lip. And nobody but *nobody* can convince you that *that* is beautiful!

Okay, so stuff like this happens. How do we deal with it?

√ CHECK YOURSELF OUT

Wash your face and don't put lotions, creams, or makeup on it. Now get in front of that mirror again, and take this "skin survey." Under each statement, circle the response that best fits the you-nique you.

1. *Let's talk zits. On my face I have*
    a. no pimples at all.
    b. a couple blackheads or pimples here and there.

c. some areas where I'm broken out.

d. about a zillion zits all over!

If you answered:

a. You're lucky. Be prepared
though, okay? Pimples
could happen anytime because as
you get older, your body will produce more oil
and your hormones will kick into high gear. That
oil combines with bacteria to clog up your pores.
Presto—pimples! Since you have ninety-four oil
glands per square inch of skin, the number of
possible zits boggles the mind.

b. Don't freak. Everybody gets a blemish at some point.
Keep your face clean, and do not pick at even one
pimple. Seriously. The oils and bacteria on your
hands, no matter how clean they are, can turn an
innocent whitehead into a big breakout and may
even leave a scar. Leave the thing alone, and it'll
go away.

c. Don't let it get to you. A breakout on one or two
parts of your face is easy to prevent or at least
improve. Besides keeping your face clean and your
hands away from it, think about what might be
adding more oil and bacteria to that part of your
skin. If the breakout is on your forehead, your bangs
might be the culprit. Keep your hair extra clean,
don't use gels or sprays on your bangs, and maybe
get the hair off your face until it clears up. If you
wear glasses and pimples appear on the bridge of

your nose, be sure to clean your specs daily. Chin zits? Check out your habits. Do you rest your chin in your hands when doing homework? Do you touch your face a lot? Keep your hands extra clean while you're trying to retrain yourself.

d. You are not a gross, disgusting, dirty person! You just have acne, which is a skin condition common in the tween and teen years. You can't help that you have acne (even a family history of acne can contribute to it), but you can make it less painful for yourself.

- Keep your skin very clean, but don't scrub it hard. Scrubbing or overdrying will only irritate your skin more.
- Try a special facial cleanser for acne from the drugstore. Products that contain benzoyl peroxide or salicylic acid are good, but you might want to test some on the inside of your wrist before putting it on your face. If you get a rash on your wrist, don't use it.
- If your acne really gets out of control—it's painful and it's upsetting you—ask your mom or dad to take you to a dermatologist (skin doctor) who can prescribe special creams or pills.
- Remember that acne usually clears up in the late teen years. That may seem like a long way away, but God will help you through till then. Really.

2. *The skin on my lips is*

    a. smooth and soft.

    b. dry and cracked.

    c. plagued with a big ol' sore (or has been before).

If you answered:

a. That's a definite blessing. Be sure to use lip balm with sunscreen when you spend a lot of time out in the sun. The skin on your lips can burn too.

b. Uncomfortable, huh? You can clear up chapped lips with lip balm. While you're at it, you might as well use one with sunscreen in it. Drink at least six glasses of water a day. Your lips are telling you your body's dried out.

c. That stinks. You have (or have had) a cold sore, also called a fever blister. It's caused by a virus, sort of like chicken pox, that will zap you when you're sick or stressed. The drugstore has products that should help. If that doesn't work, ask your doctor to prescribe something stronger.

What About Makeup?

You may have seen some girls your age wearing lipstick and mascara and blush. Maybe you thought, *Um . . . isn't she a little young for that?* Or you might have thought, *Oh, am I supposed to be thinking about wearing makeup?* Or you may even have thought, *That looks good. I really want to start wearing it myself.* Yikes—you may have even thought all of those things at the same time!

If we're going to talk about the you-nique, beautiful you, these questions are worth answering. Let's ask God.

How Is This a *God Thing?*

God comes into the makeup thing this way: He says, "Honor your father and your mother, so that you may live long in the land the LORD your God is giving you" (Exodus 20:12).

You have to live with your parents for a long time. If you want to live peacefully (and who doesn't?), you need to ask their permission about stuff like this.

Seriously, discuss with your mom and dad when you'll be allowed to wear makeup. Parents usually have some pretty good reasons for wanting their daughters to wait before they go for the lipstick and eyeliner. Some of those reasons even go back to the Bible.

- Your parents might think it looks "cheap." Remember Jezebel, the cheapest chick in the Bible (the one who had God's prophets bumped off)? She used to "paint her eyes." The "bad girls" of the Bible were often described as the ones who painted up their eyes to look sly. If it isn't applied properly or in appropriate amounts, makeup can definitely make a girl look too sophisticated when she isn't or look just plain overdone.

• Your parents don't want you to get all wrapped up in the whole appearance thing. Even the prophets, like Jeremiah, used to warn against spending so much time adorning yourself that you forget what's important (Jeremiah 2:32).

• Your parents don't want you to try to look older than you are. They'd rather you just be content with your age *right now*. That's what God seems to wants too.

Listen to your parents' reasoning. If you disagree, it's okay to present your case calmly. But if you're ready to go for the gloss and the blush and they say no, remember that it isn't the end of life as you know it. You're a natural beauty. The "enhancing" that you do with makeup will come in time.

And no fair taking lipstick and powder to school and putting them on in the bathroom when your mom has already said no! Sneakiness doesn't look good on anybody.

A good compromise might be being allowed to experiment with makeup at home but not wear it out of the house. That way when it's time for public viewing, you'll be an expert. If they say yes, remember . . .

• Too much makeup is worse than none. Use makeup to draw attention to your natural beauty, not to try to change it.

• Get someone with experience to help you at first. It takes skill and practice to use makeup well.

Otherwise you could end up looking a lot like Ronald McDonald.

- Try one thing at a time. Maybe you'll be happy with just some lip gloss or a coat of mascara or a little blush.
- Don't use makeup you don't need. If you have clear skin, who needs foundation? If your cheeks are naturally rosy, skip the blush.
- Have fun experimenting, but remember that the idea is for people to see the real you—not your makeup.
- Always take makeup off after you're finished trying things out or at the end of the day, before bed.
- Don't share makeup. That isn't stingy—it's just safe.

Fun Treats for Your Skin

Taking care of your skin doesn't have to be a drag. Try treating yourself to a "skin snack" once in a while—with a grown-up's permission, of course. Here are some fun ones to try. Your mom might even want to do it with you.

Just Do It

- Mix natural plain yogurt (no flavoring) with lemon juice, and spread it on your skin. This one is good for *all* your skin, not just your face. Lie back and chill for a while.
- Use a base of yogurt and lemon juice, and spread it over your face. Then cover all but your lips and eyes with sliced strawberries or cucumbers. It's sure to give you the giggles, but your skin will feel great after fifteen or twenty minutes.

- Soak a washcloth or small towel in hot water, wring it out, and place it over your face. Repeat this until your skin starts to glow.

Talking to God About It

When you pray today, why not talk to God about your skin stuff? He wants to share everything with you—even your zit woes and your freckle freak-outs. Just spill it all, or use this guide.

God? It's me again. I just want to talk to You about taking care of this big ol' organ, my skin:

_____

Dealing with zits:

_____

The whole staying-out-of-the-sun thing:

_____

The makeup issue:

_____

Other skin stuff:

_____

Thanks for the skin You gave me, especially:

_____ .

Lily Pad

Can you imagine yourself as a sweet old lady with wrinkly skin? What do you think you'll look like?

Four

Hands 'n' Feet

How beautiful on the mountains
are the feet of those who bring good news.

ISAIAH 52:7

Everyone who believes me will be able to do
wonderful things. . . . They will also heal sick people
by placing their hands on them.

MARK 16:17–18 CEV

Your hands and feet are two of the instruments God uses most. Naturally, then, they're part of the you-nique, beautiful you. And the good news is, they're some of the fun of being a girl.

GIRLZ Want to Know

✿ *ZOOEY: I already have to take care of my hair and my skin. Now I have to worry about my hands and feet too?*

No worries. Hands and feet are easy to pamper, and it can actually be fun. There are just a couple things you'll need to do regularly:

- Give yourself a manicure once a week and a pedicure every other week, even if it's just cleaning and clipping and filing. You can do it while you're listening to music or talking on the phone or watching a good movie.
- Use moisturizer or lotion on your hands and feet after you take a shower or bath. Even young skin can dry out on those places you use so much.

❀ *LILY: It really matters what my hands and feet look like? Are you serious?*

Sure. Have you ever seen a girl with great hair, good skin, and terrific clothes—then you looked down at her hands and saw that her nails were chipped and chewed or her skin was chapped and cracked? Or have you ever been to the beach with a friend who took all kinds of care with the beach 'do and the right swimsuit but had grimy feet or hard heels? It isn't the end of the world, of course, but it makes her look sort of unfinished, right? You really need to take care of the whole you. It *all* belongs to God.

All Hands on Deck!
Just Do It

Let's go through a hand-care routine. You'll probably find all the tools you need already in your house, but if not, just skip that step and try it later when you've had a chance to get what you need.

❀ *Tools*
- nail polish remover (only if you have nail polish on already) and cotton balls
- large bowl of warm water with some mild soap mixed in
- nail brush or metal nail-cleaning thingie (usually found on nail clippers—it's the pointed instrument)
- hand lotion
- cuticle pusher, orange stick, or Q-tip
- manicure scissors or cuticle nippers
- emery board (nail file)
- if you want to polish—clear base coat, colored polish, clear top coat

❋ **Steps**

1. Remove all old polish with cotton balls soaked with nail polish remover.

2. Trim your nails with clippers if needed; then file them with the emery board. File toward the center from each side. Zigzagging back and forth—which we all naturally want to do—will weaken your nails. Make sure all your nails are the same length and the same shape. An oval is good. You can also do rounded or squarish (it's called "squoval"—weird, huh?), but just be careful not to get your nails too short. Ingrown nails are not fun.

3. Dip your hands into the warm, soapy water, and let your nails soak for a few minutes. That will make it easier to get dirt out from under them with the brush or pointy thing. Rinse well with lukewarm water, and dry really well. This quick soak also helps later when you push back the cuticles.

4. Put some hand cream or lotion on your hands, and let it sink into your skin. Wipe off any from your nails before you go to Step 5.

5. Use the cuticle pusher to gently coax the skin around your nails back off of your nails. If you have a hangnail, use the manicure scissors or cuticle nippers to gently snip it. Don't tear at your skin (and definitely don't bite at any hangnails); it can get infected easily.

If you aren't going to polish your nails, you're done. If you do want to polish, go on to Step 6.

6. Clean the lotion off your nails with remover or rubbing alcohol so the polish will stick. Using three strokes to cover your whole nail, put one layer of base coat on all your nails. Let it dry completely before you move on. Base coat is important because putting colored polish right on your nails can eventually cause them to look yellow.

7. Put on two layers of the colored polish, again using three strokes and letting it dry between coats. This might take some practice. Don't decide you're a klutz if it's a little messy at first. You can always clean up any polish that gets on the skin around your nails with a small brush or Q-tip dipped in nail polish remover.

8. Now put on one layer of top coat or sealer (a "quick-dry" top coat is great because it'll cut the drying time, especially if you're anxious to move on to the next thing). You guessed it—use three strokes.

9. It will take several hours for your nails to completely dry, so your best bet for keeping them from chipping or smudging is to do your manicure right before you go to bed or before you're going to watch a movie and have a couple hours to let them just set. Don't get your nails wet until the polish is dry. If you really need to speed up drying time, stand with your hands in the freezer for about two minutes. That will dry the surface, but it will still be a while before all the coats are entirely dry.

Getting to the Bottom of It

Why don't we do the same with your feet? Grab your pedicure equipment:

❀ *Tools*
- nail polish remover (if your toenails are painted already) and cotton balls
- nail clippers
- a basin of warm water and a towel (or you can sit on the edge of the bathtub and soak your feet)
- pumice stone
- moisturizer
- cuticle pusher, orange stick, or Q-tip
- if you're going to polish your toenails—clear base coat, colored polish, clear top coat

Here we go with the steps. (Again, if you don't have the right tool, skip that step until you have a chance to get what you need.)

❀ *Steps*
1. Remove any old polish with remover and cotton. Never paint over old polish. You'll hate how that looks.

2. Cut your toenails straight across with the clippers. Don't cut into corners trying to get an oval shape—save that for your fingernails. Cutting away the corners can cause ingrown toenails—very painful.

3. Soak your feet for ten to fifteen minutes in the warm water to soften any calluses you have. It'll feel great, kind of like pampering yourself. Be sure to dry your feet completely—between the toes too. If you get

antsy when you have to sit still that long, grab a book or do your pedi with a friend.

4. Use the pumice stone to gently rub the callused areas. That will get the dead skin off.

5. With the pointy thing on your nail clippers, clean out any dirt from under your toenails.

6. Massage your feet with moisturizer. If you're going to polish your toenails, be sure to get all the moisturizer off your nails first with remover or rubbing alcohol.

7. Use the cuticle pusher, orange stick, or Q-tip to gently nudge your cuticles back off your nails.

If you aren't going to polish your toenails, you're done. If you are, read on.

8. Put pieces of cotton or tissue between your toes to separate them so your polish won't smudge.

9. Follow the polishing steps for fingernails (steps 6–9). Look at you! You're gorgeous right down to your fingertips and toenails.

Toe Troubles and Hand Headaches?
√ CHECK YOURSELF OUT

Take off your shoes, socks, and if possible, your nail polish. (I know you may have just finished your fingernails, so you can wait for them to dry before you do this! You don't want to mess up that fresh mani.) ☺ Let's look for the common problems you may run into with hands 'n' feet:

1. How often do you wash your hands?

Hopefully you said, "A lot," because clean hands are the best protection against germs and bacteria. Always wash after using the bathroom, before you eat, when you've been petting animals, and when you come home from a shopping trip. If you have a cold or the flu or are around others who do, double the number of times you wash your hands. If possible, wash every time you blow your nose.

2. Do you bite your nails?

If you do bite, hopefully it's just your fingernails, not your toenails. Eww. If you *are* a fingernail nibbler, that's a habit you'll want to break. Not only do nails look pretty nasty when you've chewed them down to the quick, but every time you put your hands in your mouth, you're loading up with germs. Besides, jewelry—no matter how beautiful—doesn't look good on hands with bitten nails. So how do you break a longtime habit like that? It isn't easy, but try these tricks:

- Whenever your hands aren't busy, like when you're watching TV, hold on to something little, like a stone, or play with that Silly Putty you used to love when you were a little kid.
- Get some of the special bad-tasting nail polish at the drugstore that's made to help nail biters kick the habit. Beware: it *does* taste disgusting.
- Give yourself a reward when you've gone, say, five days without biting. Keep track on a calendar—and no fair cheating!
- Start giving yourself a weekly manicure, even if you have no nails to speak of. You'll be surprised at how much easier it is to keep filed, polished nails out of your mouth.

If you nibble because you're nervous, talk to a grown-up you trust about the things that are bothering you.

3. *Do you have warts on your hands or feet?*

Not terribly attractive, right? Keep in mind that warts don't look nearly as big to anyone else as they do to you. Besides, they're harmless, just caused by a virus, and usually they'll go away on their own. The drugstore sells products to help get rid of warts, but they take a month or two to work. A doctor can also remove a wart by freezing it, but the process is a little painful and leaves a scab that takes a while to disappear. Just show your mom what you have going on, and she'll be able to help you figure out what to do. Don't pick at warts; that won't help, and it may even spread the virus and cause more. And don't bother avoiding toads—they don't cause warts, no matter what anyone tells you.

4. *Is your nail polish chipped at the moment, or does it get that way a lot?*

Nail polish does chip, and as soon as yours starts, take off the polish. Naked nails definitely look better than chipped ones. If you don't have time for regular manicures to keep up with the chipping, try wearing clear or a neutral-colored polish. Chips won't show up as much, and your mani will last a little longer. Remember that it's best not to do a complete manicure more than once a week because nail polish remover can really dry out your nails and make them brittle.

5. *Do you have little bubbles in your nail polish?*

You probably shook your nail polish too much. Try rolling the bottle between your palms a couple of times instead of shaking it.

6. Are your nails themselves chipped and split, even though you don't bite them?
Your nails are just naturally soft. Bummer. But you can buy a nail hardener to put on when you do your nails. Even if you do use one, be kind to your nails—don't use them as little crowbars or scrapers.

7. Do you have tiny white spots under your nails?
Not to worry. Those are just bruises that'll grow out. That just happens because fingers get a lot of use!

8. Are your nails so long they get in your way?
If you're blessed with hard nails that grow long and don't break, it can be fun to see how long you can grow them, but that isn't practical and doesn't look that wonderful. Somebody once said, "If your pinkie nail is long enough to spear an olive, your nails are too long." Sounds like a good rule of thumb (and every other finger)!

9. Are your feet on the puffy side?
Take the time to put them up for a while every day. It's a great thing to do while reading or talking on the phone. Also, don't sit cross-legged. That slows down the flow of blood to your legs and feet and can cause swollen ankles.

10. Do your feet, well, smell bad?
That can definitely be embarrassing! Once you've got some foot odor, nothing but a good wash will take it away, so prevention is best. To keep your feet stinkless, try these things:

- Always wear clean cotton or wool socks. Those are natural fibers that absorb sweat, which is what makes your feet give off that delicious aroma in the first place.

- Wear shoes made of natural materials like leather or canvas. Those will let your feet breathe, while shoes made out of man-made materials such as plastic are definite stench producers.
- Get the odor out of your shoes by sprinkling baking soda or one of the commercial foot/shoe powders you can buy at the drugstore in them and leaving it there overnight. When you shake out your kicks in the morning, they'll be stink-free.
- Try not to wear sneakers all the time; they're the biggest smelly-feet culprits.

11. Do your feet just plain hurt?

If you find yourself taking off your shoes every chance you get (in church, at the movies, in restaurants!), you're probably wearing uncomfortable shoes.

Try to get your feet measured at a shoe store because your feet are still growing. Have both feet measured—some people have two different sizes. (And that doesn't make them freaks.) Walk around in the shoes you're about to buy to be sure they don't rub you the wrong way. Don't buy shoes that are too small, even if the salesperson tells you they'll stretch. They won't! Too big is just as bad.

Check out the heels on your shoes. Flats should have a three-quarter-inch heel—they shouldn't be perfectly flat. High heels are fun on special occasions if you have permission, but don't wear them all day—and don't let them be too high. Really high heels throw your spine out of whack—and besides, they're really more appropriate for when you're a little older. When your heels run down, have them repaired. That'll help foot comfort too.

If the soles feel thin, use foam insoles or foot pads for more cushioning. Otherwise, it's like walking barefoot on a concrete floor. Yikes! Instant foot pain! Get the tired feeling out of your feet by putting two tablespoons of Epsom salts in two quarts of warm water and resting your feet in there for as long as the water is warm. Then massage gently. Yeah, baby . . .

12. Do you have blisters on your feet?
Blisters are spots that form where your shoes rub against your skin. Usually they start with a bubble that pops or tears open and leaves a raw place. Don't pop the blister yourself. Instead, put a Band-Aid over it to protect it until it heals, removing it at night so the blister can get air and heal faster. Then be sure to always wear the right shoes for the right activity. For instance, sneakers are better than dressy flats for long walks.

13. Do you have red, scaly patches between your toes and on the bottoms of your feet?
You probably have a common fungus called athlete's foot. They call it that because it grows on warm, moist surfaces like locker room floors, pools, and public showers. To prevent athlete's foot, wear flip-flops or shower shoes when in those places. Dry your feet really well after you shower or swim, especially between your toes. Wear shoes that let your feet breathe, and don't wear the same shoes all the time. To get rid of itchy athlete's foot, get yourself an antifungal powder, spray, or cream at the drugstore. It's easy to treat.

14. Do you have a painful flat wart on the bottom of either of your feet that hurts especially when you walk barefoot?

That's called a plantar wart, which hurts because the weight of your body is pushing it into your skin. A doctor can remove it if it really hurts you to walk.

Talking to God About It

What? You want me to talk to God about my hands and feet? Sure. Remember, God cares about all *of you. Think about it in terms of what He made your hands and feet to* do.

Dear _____ (your favorite name for God),
    I'm getting a little _____ by all this talk about manicures and pedicures! Will You help me take care of my hands and feet so I can be you-niquely beautiful and healthy?
    The most important things I do with my fingers are (play the piano? eat peanut butter out of the jar?) _____
_____.
    The most important things I do with my hands are (show the teacher I know the answers? clap at my brothers' soccer games?) _____
_____.
    The most important things I do with my toes are (pick up socks when I'm too lazy to lean over?) _____
_____.
    The most important things I do with my feet are (walk to school? dance with my dog?) _____
_____.
    God, will You especially help me with _____
_____? And most of

all, will You help me fold my hands in prayer
and walk the path You've laid out for me?
  Amen. Amen!

Lily Pad

If you had to name each of your fingers and toes,
what would their names be?

Five

When Beauty
Gets Hairy

Now, son of man, take a sharp sword and use it as a barber's razor to shave your head and your beard.

EZEKIEL 5:1

Shave? Me?

At some point, you'll probably start shaving. Now? Well, *maybe*.

Ever since American women started wearing skirts above the ankle and dresses without sleeves, they've been removing the hair from their legs and armpits to give themselves a cleaner, more ladylike look. Not everybody does it. In Europe, for instance, it isn't unusual to go to a beach and see plenty of leg and pit hair, and nobody seems to think it's funky.

If hair hasn't started growing under your arms or the hair below your knees hasn't gotten thicker than it used to be, it will eventually. Then you'll need to decide whether you want to shave or not. If you think you'd like to be hairless in those spots, ask your mom if you can shave.

How Is This a *God Thing*?

Like wearing makeup, shaving is one of those things a grown-up needs to approve. Some parents might not want you to grow up too fast, and leg shaving is a pretty sophisticated thing. Some are leery of turning you loose with a razor! Still other parents may warn you that once you start, the hair that grows back in will be more stubbly, and then you'll feel like you have to shave. Whatever her reason, if your mom says no, it stands. You gotta honor her wisdom for you; that's why God gave you parents. Besides, your mom probably won't make you go hairy forever. Try asking her again in another six months.

If She Says Go for It

Shaving's *a lot* easier than doing pre-algebra or applying eyeliner. Let's walk through it.

Just Do It

- Shave in the shower or bath because your hair will be at its softest when it's wet.
- Put a bunch of shaving cream or gel (or soap) on your armpits or legs.
- Use a new and clean razor. (Believe it or not, it's safest to use a new, sharp razor. You're less likely to nick yourself.) It's best to have your own, and those disposable ones are pretty inexpensive. Don't borrow your dad's. That's a good way to start World War III!
- Start at the top of your armpits and work down with short, downward strokes and then a few short upward strokes. The hair under your arms grows in several different directions, so you'll have to look closely while you're doing it. On legs, start at the bottom and pull the razor up your leg in long, smooth strokes. Be careful around ankles and knees, where it's easy to cut yourself. You don't have to press very hard, especially with a new razor.
- A lot of girls shave their legs only below their knees. The hair above the knees is usually pretty fine and doesn't always need shaving.
- Stop to rinse your razor often so it doesn't get globbed up with hair and soap. Rinse the razor when you're all finished, before putting it away.
- Rinse well. Dry well. Put lotion on your legs and deodorant or an antiperspirant on your armpits. You're good to go.

De-Hairing Hints
GIRLZ Want to Know

❉ *LILY: I get these little red bumps when I shave. It looks worse than it did when it was hairy!*

Razor burn city! Lily, did you remember to wet the hair before you started and to use a good amount of shaving cream or soap? Shaving dry will break you out in a rash faster than poison ivy. Never shave dry—ouch!

❉ *RENI: How often do I have to change out these disposable plastic razors anyway?*

Replace it after you've used it two or three times. That may seem wasteful, but a sharp blade is the secret to a smooth shave. That's why those dispos-able razors come in packs with lots in them.

❉ *ZOOEY: I tried shaving my legs, and I ended up with a bloody mess. My mom said I'm not allowed to try again until I'm fourteen!*

You need to listen to your mom. Next time you try shaving, whenever that is, make sure you use a sharp blade. It's a dull blade that causes nicks. Go gently and slowly—don't press hard. And be extra careful in places where bones stick out. Don't worry. You'll get the hang of it.

❉ *SUZY: I cut myself sometimes, and I can't get it to stop bleeding. Could I bleed to death?*

Probably not. Just rinse off the cut with clear water, dry it up with a tissue, and put a Band-Aid on it. Then read what I told Zooey above about preventing bloodletting while shaving!

❊ *KRESHA: My mom won't let me shave my legs, and I feel like a gorilla. What can I do? I'm afraid of being teased at school.*

First of all, you may feel like a gorilla, but I'd be willing to bet you don't *look* like one. Keep in mind that everybody else your age is so busy thinking about their own "stuff" they probably aren't even looking at your legs, hairy or not. If it makes you feel better about the way you look, wear pants, tights, or long skirts whenever you can. If you are wearing a shorter skirt or shorts, try not to think about your legs or draw attention to them by trying to hide them. Remember, God-confidence is beautiful no matter what. Even hairy legs can't change that. In a few months, ask your mom again. In the meantime, be as responsible and well-groomed as you can so that it will seem natural to her that you start shaving your legs. Whining about it won't help that image. Believe me! As for the teasing, the best answer is: "You know, that never would have occurred to me."

Talking to God About It

Try a prayer like this when you pray today. You never know where God may take you!

God? This shaving thing is (or isn't) a big deal to me because _____.

    Maybe I ought to be concentrating on some other things as well. I'm going to close my eyes and lie back and just listen for You for a little while. Will You help me use this quiet time to know what else You want me to be thinking about and doing in addition to things like shaving my legs? After all, I want to be you-niquely beautiful, inside and out.

Lily Pad

What's the funkiest spot on your body where you have hair? Write about how funny that is!

Six

Clothesline

She is clothed in fine linen and purple. . . .
She is clothed with strength and dignity.

PROVERBS 31:22, 25

So You Want to Look Good in Your Clothes?

The best way to look great is to know your body right now and wear clothes that play up your best features and feel good on you. Not your sister, your best friend, or the model on the front of *Seventeen* magazine. You-nique, beautiful you. Let's talk about how.

GIRLZ Want to Know

❀ *ZOOEY: How come Ashley and Marcie and Reni can wear those capri pants and look so cute, but when I put them on, everybody laughs?*
Because Ashley's and Marcie's and Reni's bodies are theirs, not yours. Not everybody looks great in capris. Of course, people shouldn't laugh at you, and if you feel good in capri pants, you could just ignore the teasers, remembering that *they* are the "fools." But it might be easier for you, and a lot more fun, to decide what kind of pants *do* look good on you and wear those. Get a grown-up to go to a store with you, and get a pile of different styles of pants and try them all on. Which ones make you smile at yourself in the mirror? Which ones can you really move around in the way you like to? Those are the ones to wear. And wear them proudly. You are you-niquely beautiful.

❀ *KRESHA: I have little bitty shoulders and enormous hips! No clothes look good on me. I always look like a walking pear!*
You probably don't actually look like a "walking pear" or any other fruit. Remember what we said about our pictures of our own bodies? But . . . if you want things to look more balanced, then wear white or light colors on

top. Full tops or ones with pockets will even things out. The opposite goes for girls with nice broad shoulders and slim hips. They can get a balance by wearing loose pants or skirts with simple, streamlined tops and button-downs. Pretty cool, huh?

❋ *LILY: I'm so tall! I'm trying to accept me just the way God made me. But sometimes my clothes look kinda silly.* Don't wear anything short, Lily, like really short skirts or rib-tickling tops. Big ol' heels probably won't help if you already feel like you're towering above the crowds. Then straighten your shoulders, hold your head high, and love being stately.

❋ *RENI: I have the opposite problem. I'm way short, and some of my clothes make me look like even more of a shrimp.* Nothing wrong with being short. You're petite. Dainty. Pleasantly elfish. If you'd like to feel a little taller, just for fun, wear the same color clothes from your hat to your shoes. It'll look like you've added inches. Don't wear anything that "cuts you in half"—like a big ol' wide belt at your waist or a short top that's a different color than your skirt or pants.

✓ CHECK YOURSELF OUT

Let's get in front of that mirror again and have some fun finding out more about you-nique you. Look at yourself (you're getting to like you now, aren't you?), and answer these questions. Then let's see what the answers tell you.

What are your three very best features? Do you have curly hair, sparkly eyes, and great legs? Or is your trio your big smile, broad shoulders, and tiny waist? Write yours here.

1.

2.

3.

Clothes Tip: Use "attention-catchers" like these on or near those features:

- light, bright colors that you love
- big patterns and bold textures like large plaids or big knits
- shiny fabrics like satin
- glitter, sequins, or rhinestones
- fancy details like ruffles, lace, or embroidery
- jewelry and scarves

For example, on that tiny waist, wear fun belts. On that curly hair? Go for bright-colored hair ties or shiny barrettes. Get the idea?

What are the three features you aren't as happy with? (Remember that God loves 'em all!) Are you self-conscious about your nose? Do you feel as if your long arms are everywhere? Do you wish your calves were more slender? Write your three here, but be *kind* to yourself in the way you describe them!

1.

2.

3.

Clothes Tip: Don't use the attention-catchers on or near any feature you want to play down.

For example, bright red tights aren't the best choice if you don't want eyes drawn to your calves. A hat that points right to your nose won't draw attention *away* from it.

Which of these best describes the things you like to do? You might be a combination of some of these, so if that's the case, number them 1, 2, and 3, with 1 being the one you are most of the time.

a. Anything that involves sports or just being active, like softball or swimming or riding my bike. I hate to sit around.

b. Anything that makes me think, like reading, writing, playing board games, doing stuff at the computer, or even watching really good movies. As long as I'm using my mind, I'm happy.

c. Anything that makes me either laugh or cry, like reading, writing, watching movies, playing pretend games, daydreaming, or being in plays. Let me feel emotions, and I'm good to go.

Clothes Tip: Not only is it more fun to wear clothes that make you look your best, but it's a blast to wear things that match your *style*. We can change styles as often as we want—it's fun to experiment. But when it comes to really feeling like *you*, you may want to think about wearing clothes that tell who you are.

If you answered a, the sporty style might suit you best. Don't fill up your closet with too many frills because you're probably most comfortable in things you can really move around in. That might mean jeans and T-shirts or fun flip-flops in every color or even swingy knit dresses with leggings.

If you answered b, think about the tailored look. Just remember that *tailored* doesn't mean boring! It could mean cargo pants instead of jeans. Maybe for you it's great sweaters and pleated plaid skirts. You're just the type who can pull off a pair of leather-looking boots.

If you answered c, chances are you like anything romantic. Wear ruffles and lace if you want—even if nobody else is doing it. Grab that embroidered vest your sister is about to give to Goodwill. Put on pink socks with your tennis shoes. You're a dreamer, so dream up outfits that are completely you.

Just Do It

You don't need a lot of clothes to get the look you want. You can probably get it with the stuff you already have. Take an afternoon when you can pull everything out of your closet and put it on your bed. As you put each item back into your closet, play around with it, and ask yourself these questions:

- How many other things does this piece of clothing go with? You can wear those red shorts with white, blue, and red prints of course, but what about yellow? Or green? A piece of jewelry or a hair gizmo that has those same two colors will tie it together, and you've got a smashing outfit that is totally you! Remember, items in an outfit don't always have to match; they just have to *go* together.

- If this item doesn't shout your style all by itself, what can you do with it to get it there? Did you ever think of wearing that silky skirt you think is too fussy with your denim jacket? You can be sporty *and* dressed up.
- Does the piece of clothing not actually fit you right? Or do you just know that no matter what you do with it, it still isn't going to be you? Put everything like that into a box to give to a worthy cause. It's bound to be *somebody's* fit and style.

What Would God Think of Your Clothes?

He cares about my *clothes*? Yes! He does!

How Is This a *God Thing*?

Your clothes tell as much about you as anything you tell people about yourself. If you're into a hipster thing or a dark and edgy thing, that might tell people you think that basically everything is a downer or you're trying to tick off all the adults—even if that's not how you really feel. If you run around in short shorts and itty-bitty tops, you're screaming, *"I'm a boy chaser!"* without even opening your mouth.

What *does* God want us to say with our clothes? He spells it out for us in the Bible. (Isn't that just like Him?)

Just in case you were thinking about forgetting the whole clothes thing altogether and joining a nudist colony, remember that God *does* insist that people wear clothes. He made the very first ones for Adam and Eve:

*The L*ORD *God made garments of skin for
Adam and his wife and clothed them.*

GENESIS 3:21

He wants your clothes to say you're a girl. I don't think He means we women can't put on a ball cap and sweatshirt, but we do need to show the world that we are you-niquely feminine. He wants your clothes to say you're a woman who worships Him. That means He doesn't want you to dress just so everybody will look at you:

*I also want women to dress modestly, with decency
and propriety . . . with good deeds, appropriate
for women who profess to worship God.*

1 TIMOTHY 2:9-10

He wants your clothes to say that you don't need the most expensive, the flashiest, the most bizarre, or the most popular label. He wants your clothes to let your true beauty come from the inside:

*Your beauty should not come from outward
adornment. . . . Instead, it should be that of your
inner self, the unfading beauty of a gentle and quiet
spirit, which is of great worth in God's sight.*

1 PETER 3:3-4

He wants them to say, "I respect myself and my God." That means looking the very best you can, because you're happy to be you:

*She is clothed with strength and dignity;
she can laugh at the days to come.*

PROVERBS 31:25

But *Everybody* Has One!

Sometimes it feels like there's nothing worse than not having the most hip thing everybody else has. It makes you feel like a loser, right? Like you're totally out of it. Like the biggest geek since . . .

Well, you get the idea. And believe it or not, so does your mom. Girls have been begging their moms for what's hot as far back as history goes. Girls in the 1920s wanted short skirts (in the twenties, that meant above the ankle!) and bobbed hair, and they whined to be allowed to wear their galoshes unbuckled because everybody else was doing it. Girls in the 1960s hankered for love beads and tie-dyed stuff. Girls in the 1980s wanted three pairs of socks to match each outfit and wore them all at the same time! Look at some photographs of your mom when she was your age. Can you stand it? No telling what *your* daughter will try to get you to buy for her!

It's natural to want to fit in. There isn't even anything wrong with it—unless doing it is going to mess up something else that's much more important. Try following these guidelines when you're shopping for clothes with the grown-up in your life.

Things You Should Avoid Whining for While Shopping

1. Anything you know your family can't afford. If you see your mom scrambling for change in the bottom of her purse at the grocery store,

don't ask for the tennis shoes with all the bells and whistles on them.

2. Anything your mom or dad has already said no to. If you handle their decision in a mature way, the answer might be yes the next time you ask for something.

3. Anything you know is bad news, no matter how cool everybody else thinks it is. Maybe anybody who's anybody is wearing a necklace with a skull on it, but why even bring it up when you know it's dark?

4. Anything trendy if you have a whole closet full of trendy stuff that went out of style in a week and hasn't been worn since.

But I Wanna Be Cool!

- So start your own trends—be retro; be funky; be different. Get all your Christian friends to wear crosses. Do cool things with your church camp T-shirts.
- Be so you-niquely you that no one cares whether you have Hollister or a Walmart brand. If you look around, you'll discover that the really cool people are the ones other people like because of who they are, not what they wear.
- If money's the only problem, work around the house and for neighbors to earn the cash to buy that very *now* thing you want. Chances are, when you get to the checkout counter and have to part with your hard-earned money, you'll think hard about whether that "cool" thing is really worth it.

Talking to God About It

Dear _____ (your favorite name for God),

We talked about a lot of stuff in this chapter. Will You help me sort it out? Will You help me figure out who I really am so I can reflect that in the things I wear?

Will You help me accept my body and be happy looking my best instead of trying to look someone else's best?

Will You help me make the most of everything I have?

Will You help me show that I love and respect myself and You even in the things I wear?

Will You help me to be accepted for who I am, instead of for how many of the latest clothes I wear?

Thanks, God. I knew I could count on You.

Love, _____

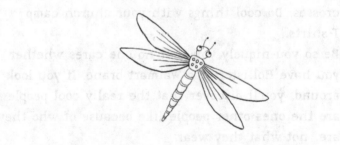

Lily Pad

Describe your dream outfit—the perfect ensemble that would show you exactly as you are, fit perfectly, show off all your best features, and be fun to wear. Describe it in detail, head to toe.

Describe your dream outfit · · ·

Make it an outfit God would love!

Don't Trash Your Temple!

Do you not know that your body is a temple of the Holy Spirit, who is in you, whom you have received from God? . . . Therefore honor God with your body.

1 CORINTHIANS 6:19-20

How Is This a *God Thing?*

Because your *body* is a God thing. Not only did God create your body, but it's filled with the Holy Spirit. Doing anything but taking care of it and respecting it and using it for God is like dumping a load of garbage in the middle of a church sanctuary.

Usually when we talk about taking care of our temple-bodies, we're thinking about healthy food and exercise and not smoking or using illegal drugs. But "trashing your temple" on the outside is just as upsetting to God as messing it up on the inside. Some of the things that are considered cool right now are the same as painting graffiti on the front of the temple—*your* temple.

GIRLZ Want to Know About Body Piercing

❀ *ZOOEY: My mom won't let me get my ears pierced. She says I'll look too old for my age—and besides, she says that, knowing me, they'll probably get infected.*

Once again, you need to honor your mom by doing—and not doing—as she asks. As for infections, they sometimes do happen with ear piercings. If and when the time comes, go to a place with a reputation for doing good, clean work. (Don't let a friend do it with an ice cube and a sewing needle!) Then keep your new holes clean with the

solution the store will give you. Keep your earrings clean too. Until Mom says yes, show her how capable you are of taking care of the rest of your body. She might change her mind sooner than you think.

❀ *LILY: My parents let me get my ears pierced, but they said a flat-out no to having my tongue, nose, or belly button done. What's the difference?*

For one thing, although ear piercing is pretty common today, putting holes in other parts of your body for jewelry still carries the look and feel of someone really trying to draw attention to herself—and not always for the best reasons. Girls with pierced noses, eyebrows, or tongues tend to look rebellious and disrespectful, even if they aren't. They sometimes set themselves up for unnecessary battles that way.

Another reason is that ear piercing doesn't really interfere with other bodily functions. Your earlobes just kind of hang there. But your nose and your tongue have jobs to do, and a post or ring stuck in there can get in the way.

Besides all that, we've been talking about the whole beautiful you. A big ol' rhinestone in your eyebrow doesn't say, "Look at the you-niquely beautiful me." More than likely, it says, "Look at my eyebrow!" And you want to send that message because . . . ?

GIRLZ Want to Know About Tattoos

❀ *RENI: I heard that getting a tattoo really hurts. Is that true?*

It's done with an electric tattoo machine, which involves a needle piercing the surface of your skin 80–150 times per second, injecting permanent dye into your skin. Does it sound like *that* would hurt?!?

❁ *SUZY: I heard getting a tattoo could be dangerous. Is it?*
You heard right. Any time anyone injects a needle into your skin, there's a danger of passing germs and bacteria into your body. We're not just talking about getting a rash here. A person can get hepatitis (in extreme cases even AIDS) from a contaminated needle. That doesn't mean this always happens, but it can, so we need to think about it. Good, responsible tattoo artists use sterile procedures. But why chance it for a picture in your skin—and a picture you're stuck with forever?

❁ *LILY: You can't get rid of a tattoo, can you?*
It's tough. It requires another procedure with lasers that most people don't want to go through, and the removal process is expensive and painful. So why get a tattoo in the first place?

❁ *KRESHA: Would it be all right to get the kind you just stick on?*
Is it all right with—you guessed it—your parents? They might not like even the idea of a tattoo, real or fake. Leviticus 19:28 does say, "Do not . . . put tattoo marks on yourselves." Of course, Leviticus 19:27 also says, "Do not . . . clip off the edges of your beard." Just check it out with your folks before you start sticking things on.

83

Sometimes I Just Want to Be Different!

Have you ever gone into a salon and looked at some of the hairstyle books? Aren't those 'dos bizarre sometimes? Hair sticking straight up or straight out or all pointing toward the front like a bunch of arrows?

And have you ever thought, *I'd like to do that, just go to extremes*?

It would be safer with clothes, of course, because you can always change them. You're sort of stuck with a hairstyle or a piercing or a tattoo . . . Get my drift?

Before you go any further with that daydream, let's talk to God about it.

Talking to God About It

Pray this little prayer:

Dear God, I love You. I want to be exactly who You want me to be. I want to be you-niquely beautiful, but I don't want to distract anybody from seeing You in me. When people look at me, I want them to be reminded of how good You are, what a great job You did making me. I want the way I look on the outside to be a God thing. Thanks for making me.
Amen.

Now think about going to extremes again.

84

✓ CHECK YOURSELF OUT

We've been talking about being you-niquely you. But there is a difference between looking like *you* and not worrying about what everybody else is doing AND putting something on *just* to get attention.

Let's check that out. Read each of these stories. If any one reminds you of something you've done or are doing now, put a check mark next to it. Then give it some serious thought and prayer. Talk to your parents about it. Are you going a little extreme, or is that just an expression of that very special you?

Keely decided it was going to be her trademark to always have a teddy bear sticking out of her clothes someplace. The bear's head would be peeking out between the buttons on her flannel shirt or poking from the waistband of her jeans. People started referring to her as "the Teddy Bear Girl."

Jessie really wanted to have her head shaved so she could feel like her body was her own. She nagged about it so much that her parents finally said, "Go for it." At first it was cool having people she didn't even know come up to her and ask her why she did it, because then she could say, "Because I wanted to." But that got old, and she wished everybody would just deal with it.

Emmy got bored in school a lot and would draw on herself with felt-tip markers. When everybody told her how neat that was, she started doing it all the time.

There was a heart on one cheek, a star on the other, and sometimes entire scenes on her arms and legs.

Christie wanted to set a trend, so she started wearing only pink. She was rosy—from headband to flip-flops. It caught on with some of her friends, until they looked like bottles of Pepto-Bismol when they were together. Others picked their own colors and wore just purple or totally yellow. Still others started a rumor that Christie was the leader of some weird cult.

Lily Pad

If I wanted to show the very most unique part of me, in a God-thing way, using my appearance, I would . . .

Eight

What If I Have to Put Up With . . . ?

Leah had weak eyes, but Rachel was lovely in form, and beautiful.

GENESIS 29:17

Glasses? Braces? Becoming Amazon woman? I don't want to look like a weirdo!

Of course you don't. No one does. But there isn't an appearance "flaw" that can't be overcome. If might even end up being the best part of you!

How Is This a *God Thing*?

Go back to that mirror we've been using. Take another long look at your friend in there (you-nique you), and focus on that physical thing you're struggling with—those glasses or those braces or that birthmark.

Now read below what God has to say about it. Every time you see a blank, write your "hang-up" in there.

> *[A person with] _____ may eat the most holy food of . . . God.*
> LEVITICUS 21:22

So in the first place, when it comes to whether He loves you or not, God couldn't care less whether you wear glasses or have braces or sport the biggest wart in the history of the universe. "Come on in," He says!

> *Praise be to . . . the God of all comfort, who comforts us in all our _____.*
> 2 CORINTHIANS 1:3-4

Grown-ups may tell you glasses or braces or funky moles are no big deal, but God understands how hard that is right now. Go to Him—He's there with the comfort.

Neither _____ *nor* _____ . . .
will be able to separate us from the love of
God that is in Christ Jesus our Lord.

ROMANS 8:39

So do those things really matter so much when you get right down to it?

Man looks at the _____, *but*
the Lord *looks at the heart.*

1 SAMUEL 16:7

So concentrate on who you are *inside.* Sure, other people may still stare at your ten thousand freckles or tease you about being tall, but working on your spiritual self will make you less self-conscious. And eventually, people will even start to comment, "You're getting to be so pretty." Most of them won't even know why.

Look at you in the mirror again—the you who knows she's loved, the you who realizes those knobby knees don't mean squat to the beautiful person. You gotta love her, don't you?

Now do her a favor and let that "flaw" become an asset. Read on . . .

GIRLZ Want to Know About Glasses

🌸 *ZOOEY: I think I might need glasses, but I don't know if I want to wear them. Won't they make me look ugly?*
First of all, your eyesight comes first. If you have any of these symptoms, ask your parents to have your eyes examined by an optometrist. You may need glasses if . . .

- you get headaches from reading
- you have to squint your eyes to see things, either up close or far away
- you sometimes have double vision

And, no, glasses don't necessarily have to make you look ugly. They're actually pretty trendy and cool these days. The optometrist or eye center where you go will have a selection of frames and a wall full of mirrors. Experiment with as many colors, shapes, and sizes as you want until you find something that makes you smile at yourself. They say there's a hat to suit everyone; I'm sure that's true of glasses too.

❀ *SUZY: I have to wear glasses when I read, and I feel ridiculous! I'm just about the only one in the class who has them.*

Lots of people's eyes start to change around your age and on into their teens. Pretty soon, as you look around, you'll see more and more people whipping them out to see the board or read their textbooks. Right now, you're unique, so pick out the cutest pair you can find, and be as adorable as you are!

❀ *LILY: My mom makes me wear sunglasses on bright days, but the ones she bought me make me look like a mosquito or something!*

Your mom's right. Sunglasses will protect your eyes from ultraviolet rays. It sounds like you just have the wrong style. Your best bet for sunglasses or regular specs are frames that don't extend past the sides of your face. Lots of styles are popular right now—aviators, bold frames, metal frames, even funky colors. Ask your mom if you can try a different pair and see if they aren't fun. The right sunglasses can give you a mysterious, classy air.

🌸 *RENI: If I need help with my vision, I'd rather get contact lenses than glasses.*

Contacts are great and don't change the way you look, but they do require care and cleaning, and they can be tough to get used to at first. However, if your eye doctor and your parents think you're ready for them, then maybe you can give them a try.

GIRLZ Want to Know About Braces

🌸 *RENI: I just found out I have to get braces. I can almost hear the boys at school calling me "Tinsel Teeth" and "Metal Mouth."*

Remember what to do about teasing: ignore and pray. And besides, braces aren't so bad anymore. They come in colors, and so do the rubber bands you might have to use. We're talking everything from baby blue to neon. Or you can get clear braces, which are practically invisible until someone gets up close. Get some cool ones, and then smile, smile, smile! You'll dazzle the daylights out of those teasers. Plus, how many other kids are dealing with braces and retainers right now too? You're not alone in the world of orthodontics.

🌸 *KRESHA: People with braces usually look all yellow-toothed and stuff. I don't want that!*

It doesn't have to be that way if you take care of your teeth and braces. Brush after every meal or snack. (You might start a trend in the bathroom at school. Get yourself a neat toothbrush and a miniature tube of toothpaste, and keep them in a cool zippered bag in your backpack.) At least once a day, really go for it with the cleaning, maybe with an electric toothbrush (you can get them at any drugstore or even the grocery store) or some dental floss. Not only will you keep your smile shiny now, but you'll avoid gunky-looking teeth when the braces come off. Avoid foods that will stick to your teeth and practically have to be pried off with a crowbar—like caramel apples and Gummi bears.

GIRLZ want to Know: *What If I'm Too Tall?*

Or too short? What if I'm way behind the other girls physically? Or, sometimes worse, way ahead?

We've talked before about not comparing yourself to other people, but it's hardest when the other girls are showing off their long legs at a sleepover, or when no boy wants to be paired up with you in folk dancing because he doesn't want to look in your belly button. We need a little more reassurance from God on that.

Talking to God About It

The first thing you need to do is vent to God. He knows what's on your mind and likes to hear you say it. Write your gripe (or your multiple complaints) on these lines, the way you'd like to say them to the Big Dad.

God, I know You knew best when You made me, but could we talk about my _____?
It really bothers me because _____.
Thanks for listening. Amen.

Now you try listening. Find a quiet place (that's tough in some houses!), sit back, and close your eyes. Just be with God for a few minutes. Try to chase all other thoughts out of your head except the ones about God. Relax. Think God. Breathe God in. Enjoy a little P-and-Q (peace and quiet) with the Guy who made you.

Try that every day for several days—praying and then getting quiet. In the meantime, during the rest of your day, be alert for God's answers in things other people say, in things you read in your Bible, in new thoughts that come into your head. Girls who've tried it report that God has told them things like:

- "It's a process. You didn't pop out in the delivery room with all your teeth and hair, right? Give Me time to let you grow into yourself."
- "It isn't always going to be like this. Boys will grow taller. Other girls will grow bigger chests and catch up. You might feel like a sore thumb now, but give Me time. I have a separate growing plan for each of you."
- "It's a big deal now because it's all new. But very soon you're going to stop caring so much about whether you're the most flat-chested girl in the class. You can hurry that along by concentrating on other things—like *Me*!"
- "I happen to like you exactly the way you are this minute. Because you hate it when other people tease you about being short, you hardly ever tease anyone else. In fact, you give people compliments whenever you get the chance. Would you be like that if I hadn't made you the way you are?"

When you discover what God's saying to you—and you will if you pay attention—write it here. You may want to look back at it from time to time.

God said: _____

Just Do It

Below Lily has written down her "Big Ugliness," as she calls it—the one thing about herself that really bothers her most. Then she prayed, like you did, and she's come up with four things she's going to do to make her "flaw" a cool thing to have. Look back through this chapter and see if you can't do the same for yours.

🌸 *Lily Robbins*

My Big Ugliness is my height. I'm like the Empire State Building in a classroom full of Fisher-Price playhouses. I am totally serious!

But I've prayed and I've read my Bible and I've read this book, and I think there are things I can do about it.

1. *I am so not going to pay any attention to Shad Shifferdecker when he teases me. He can call me Robbins Tower all he wants, but I'm just going to ignore him. When it hurts my feelings, I'm going to vent to God—and pray that Shad will actually grow up someday.*

2. *I made a list of all the good things about being tall—like I can always reach stuff, I can always see over the crowd, people think I'm older than I am and don't treat me like a little kid. I keep my list in my binder so when I start to feel like Lily the Giant, I can look at it, and sometimes it helps.*

3. *I keep remembering that God made me, which means He must like me this way. It would be kind of rude to try to be different, so I'm concentrating*

on my posture, standing up really straight and tall, and all that.

4. My dad told me that when I grow into myself, I'm going to be "statuesque." I don't know exactly what that means, but I like the sound of it. Sometimes, if I have to walk up to the front of the room or something, I say to myself over and over, "I'm statuesque, I'm statuesque."

Now you try it!

My "Big Ugliness":

_____

_____

_____

_____

Things I think God wants me to do about that:

_____

_____

_____

_____

Lily Pad

When I have my own daughters, I'm going to show them pictures of me at this age and tell them how funny it was dealing with my _____.

Here's how I'm gonna tell it . . .

Nine

You Go, Girl!

*Your beauty . . . should be that of your inner self,
the unfading beauty of a gentle and quiet spirit,
which is of great worth in God's sight.*

1 PETER 3:3-4

Remember God-Confidence?

That's what this whole book has been about, right? Learning that you are a gorgeous girl because God loved you enough to make you exactly the way He wanted you to be. Knowing that gives you God-confidence—and there isn't a woman alive with that confidence who doesn't turn heads when she walks into a room. People may not know *why* you're beautiful. They may mutter to each other, "She isn't the typical definition of pretty, but there's something about her . . ."

Let's not leave our look at the you-niquely beautiful you without making sure you're on your way to having that "unfading beauty of a gentle and quiet spirit" that gives you God-confidence. (And don't let the "gentle and quiet" part scare you. Even we motormouths can have it!)

√ CHECK YOURSELF OUT

First, find out that you're already on your way. Circle the very best, *honest* answer to each of the questions on the following pages.

Have you given up dissing the way you look?
>   Yeah, baby!
>   Getting there.
>   Uh, not yet . . .

Are you now laughing at how ridiculously unreal most advertising is?
>   Yeah, baby!
>   Getting there.
>   Uh, not yet . . .

Have you stopped playing the Comparison Game?

> Yeah, baby!
> Getting there.
> Uh, not yet . . .

Have you learned how to deal with teasing?

> Yeah, baby!
> Getting there.
> Uh, not yet . . .

Do you know what is you-niquely beautiful about you?

> Yeah, baby!
> Getting there.
> Uh, not yet . . .

Are you taking good care of your hair—keeping it healthy and styled just for you?

> Yeah, baby!
> Getting there.
> Uh, not yet . . .

Are you taking good care of your skin because it's an important part of your temple?

> Yeah, baby!
> Getting there.
> Uh, not yet . . .

Are you following your parents' decisions regarding your looks?

> Yeah, baby!
> Getting there.
> Uh, not yet . . .

Are you paying attention to your hands 'n' feet too because you respect yourself enough to take care of every detail?

Yeah, baby!

Getting there.

Uh, not yet . . .

Are you wearing clothes God would love?

Yeah, baby!

Getting there.

Uh, not yet . . .

Are you avoiding trashing your temple on the outside?

Yeah, baby!

Getting there.

Uh, not yet . . .

Are you turning your biggest "flaw" into one of the best parts of you?

Yeah, baby!

Getting there.

Uh, not yet . . .

Are you learning how to talk to God about everything?

Yeah, baby!

Getting there.

Uh, not yet . . .

Are you convinced that you're beautiful?

Yeah, baby!

Getting there.

Uh, not yet . . .

Now look back at your answers.

The *Yeah, baby!* answers show that you're really making progress in those areas. Keep it up. The more you do those things, the more beautiful you're going to feel—and be.

The *Getting there* answers show where you're working and need to keep on working to get rid of junk attitudes so there's room for the truth. I'm proud of you.

The *Uh, not yet . . .* answers are pretty important. They show you what to focus on. What to pray about. What to ask your mom or some other friend you really trust to help you with. Notice that they aren't final *nos*. We are all God's works in progress. The job isn't done. At least you know what needs to happen. With God's help, you'll get there.

Final Words You Gotta Love

As you're working on all the outside things we've talked about in this book, keep reminding yourself that your God-confidence is what makes you more truly beautiful than a weekly manicure and the most expensive haircut. It's the quiet, gentle spirit that makes people wonder what your secret is.

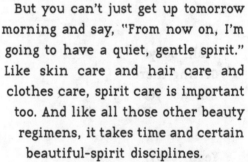

But you can't just get up tomorrow morning and say, "From now on, I'm going to have a quiet, gentle spirit." Like skin care and hair care and clothes care, spirit care is important too. And like all those other beauty regimens, it takes time and certain beautiful-spirit disciplines.

Here are a few that are guaranteed to get you nearer and nearer to the God who shapes your spirit:

- Having a quiet time with God every day, praying and listening for at least twenty minutes.
- Reading God's Word and thinking about how it applies to you right that very moment. You can make it part of your quiet time.
- Journaling, like you've started to do on your Lily Pads.
- Surrounding yourself with other beautiful Christians as your very best friends.
- Treating those friends—and everyone—the way you've learned to treat yourself.

Oh, and there's one last one. It's the very simplest thing in this book, and yet it's the one guaranteed to make you more beautiful than just about anything else you can do. Ready for it?

Smile!

It won't be hard. After all, God loves you. And you gotta love that!

Check out this excerpt from the next
nonfiction book in The Lily Series!

The Body Book

One

What's Going On in There?

Sixty queens there may be . . .
but my dove, my perfect one, is unique.

SONG OF SONGS 6:8-9

It's either happening already, or you've heard that it's going to happen.

- You're growing breasts.
- Hair is appearing in new places.
- You're sweating more.
- You've got the body odor thing going on.
- You're gaining weight or getting taller by the minute.
- Your friends are talking about starting their periods.
- You're giggling one minute and crying the next.

And in the middle of it all, you're looking in the mirror and saying, "Who are *you* and what have you done with *me*?"

This time in your life—between about eight and thirteen years old—is when more changes are happening in your body than have ever happened since that first year (when you had to triple your weight, grow teeth, and figure out how to walk!). It can be a confusing time—a time when you want to shout to your body, "What's going on in there?"

Hopefully this will be a help to you: "what's going on in there" is normal. All these changes are because of something called *puberty*—and it happens to every girl and has since God first started making females. And probably every girl has had the same questions you might be having.

GIRLZ Want to Know

🌸 *LILY: Everybody talks about "When you hit puberty . . ." What is puberty anyway?*
Puberty is the time when your body starts producing two new hormones it hasn't produced before.

❀ *RENI: Swell. So what's a hormone?*

A hormone is a chemical that's produced in a certain organ or gland and is then sent to another part of your body to go to work. The two new hormones in puberty are *estrogen* and *progesterone*.

❀ *ZOOEY: I have chemicals in my body? Why? What are they doing in there?*

They're slowly turning you into a woman.

Estrogen causes:
- the development of your breasts (time for a bra?)
- the widening of your hips (think of it as curves)
- the growth of all that extra hair in your armpits and pubic area
- the production of more oil in your skin and hair (enter pimples and greasies!)
- the thickening of the hair on your legs (break out the razor!)
- your new interest in boys (They haven't gotten any less absurd—you just don't mind as much!)

Progesterone, along with estrogen, causes and controls your period.

How Is This a *God Thing?*

You may find yourself wanting to ask God, "How come I have to go through all these pimples and all this embarrassing hair and all this crying that comes out of nowhere? Couldn't there have been a better way?"

In *our* minds, it may seem easier to wake up one day with a mature body, clear skin, and perfect coordination—but would that really be better?

People would also expect you to *act* like a full-grown woman, and where would *that* come from?

God made growth—all kinds of growth—a gradual process that takes time. The slow appearance of hair, the day-by-day way your breasts grow, the trial-and-error you have to go through with your emotions— that's all part of God's plan for you to have time to get used to the idea of becoming a woman. Hopefully by the time you look in the mirror when you're eighteen or twenty, you're going to pretty much like what you see. The trick is to make it till then, right?

That's what this book is about: helping you understand "what's going on in there" and giving you some hints on how to grow with it, physically and spiritually.

As always, there might be some obstacles, so let's try to get those out of the way right up front.

Body Blocker #1:
I'm So Far Behind Everybody Else!

Maybe you're twelve and all your friends are getting their periods and wearing bras, and you still look (and feel) like a little girl. If you have a brother who asks you, "Hey, sis, when's the breast fairy gonna come?" or you have the fear that you're never going to catch up, just remember these things:

- It isn't a contest! You'll get there at the right time for *you*.
- You are your own you-nique self. God has already planned how and when you're going to grow into that.

- Meanwhile, it's who you are *inside* that counts, anyway. If you have God-confidence, you're going to look, act, and feel just right. Concentrate on God and who He wants you to be.
- Enjoy being free of bras and maxi pads while you can!

Body Blocker #2:
I'm So Far Ahead of Everybody Else!

Maybe you're twelve and are already in a C cup and have been having periods since you were ten. And maybe as a result, you feel like a freak.

If you're suffering from nicknames like "Betty Big Boobs" or other people are expecting you to act like you're sixteen because you look like you are, perhaps thinking about these things will help you:

- While you're wishing you didn't have such a well-developed chest, other girls are looking at their flat ones and wishing they could be so lucky! And yet, wishing won't make it so. You're going to develop on the schedule God has programmed for your body.
- Remember that as your age group matures, you'll get less and less teasing because other girls will catch up, and boys won't think it's so funny to give you nicknames.
- Meanwhile, if it makes you feel more comfortable, wear clothes that play down your maturing breasts and curvy hips. It's not a matter of hiding who you are; it's a way to cut down on the teasing until everybody else grows up!
- Know that God loves you and has a plan for you, and that includes your womanly body. Let that give you

the God-confidence to walk proud. Do not, under any circumstances, be ashamed of the way you're made. It's a God thing.

Body Blocker #3:
I Just Don't Want to Grow Up

Maybe the whole idea of wearing a bra, shaving your legs, remembering to put on deodorant, and—the worst!—getting your period seems really scary to you.

Don't feel alone. A lot of girls feel that way. Remembering these things might help you:

- Every girl goes through it, so you aren't alone. Share your fears with your friends. It'll bring you all closer together.
- God makes sure you have at least one adult in your life who is willing to help you figure this stuff out. Look around. Is it your mom? Older sister or other relative? A minister, counselor, nurse, or doctor? Knowing you have someone to go to who has been there (and done that!) will make you feel less afraid.
- It helps to think of puberty as sort of a path to better and better things.
- It's *fun* being a woman! We women get to have great relationships, experience incredible adventures, know never-ending love, and—someday—have babies. But to get there someday, you have to be *here* now.

Talking to God About It

Let's start by praying. In the space below, write a letter to God, pouring out all the private, scary, embarrassing, I-don't-want-to stuff you have inside. Just get it all out there—give it to God, and rest assured that He's listening. If that's hard for you, perhaps filling in the blanks in this open letter might help.

Dear _____ (insert your favorite name for God),

I know this whole puberty thing is Your plan, but I have some problems with it. For one thing, I'm embarrassed about _____.

Besides that, I'm kind of worried about _____.

And when you get right down to it, I'm just plain scared about _____.

Will You please help me not to be too embarrassed or scared to ask _____ for help?

Will You please help me get answers to my question(s) about _____?

And most of all, please help me remember that I'm not alone—that You're there for me. I love You!

_____ (your name)

Lily Pad

My most embarrassing moment in growing up
so far has been when . . .

Printed in the USA
CPSIA information can be obtained
at www.ICGtesting.com
JSHW032004270624
65514JS00006B/25

9 781400 319480